PERSPECTIVES IN TIME

PERSPECTIVES
IN TIME

Susan H. Brown

Edited by Martha Fuller
Layout and design by Sharon E Rawlins

HERMANN PRESS
Encino, California
hermannpress20@gmail.com

ISBN # 979-8-218-43133-4

———

This book is typeset in Cardo, designed by David J. Perry. It is an old-style serif typeface and an interpretation of work by Aldus Manutius, a Renaissance printer. Display type is Futura.

Printed in the United States of America

To Murray
with all my love

CONTENTS

Preface

Old World Revisited

New World

Goodbyes

Memories

Art—Inspiration for Poems

Music

Special Children with Special Needs

Travel

Musings

There is no past we can bring back by longing for it. There is only an eternal now that builds and creates out of the past something new and better.

—Johann Wolfgang von Goethe

PREFACE

Why Write

What hubris!
My story should be preserved,
A story like millions before
And millions yet to come.
I look inside me—over and over,
I find the same lies, the same truths.
I listen to the past,
To what is gone, passed, buried.
I cry, I hurt, I remember,
I embellish, I omit, I invent.

I search for words to hide behind,
Words as proxy to that
Which is unutterable.
Words that silence the chaos,
That calm the unanswerable quest.

A testimonial filled with missing pieces.
A story without a final chapter.

WARS

Winter 1944

Ukraine 2022

February—Los Angeles 2022

February—Ukraine 2022

Never Again—Ukraine 2022

Never Again—Israel 2023

Winter 1944

The end of the war is in sight,
The end of Jewry still unaccomplished.
A cunning, clever Hungarian Jewish lawyer
And a cruel, calculating German bureaucrat
Enter a trade deal:
Money and goods in exchange for Jewish lives.
War equipment for a desperate killer,
Jews for a desperate gambler.

Mass murders continue,
Fate and privilege save a few.
The "man in the glass booth" proud
Of his actions,
Welcomes his executioners.
The "trucks for lives" savior-traitor assassinated
For his dubious and duplicitous past.

Ukraine 2022

Bombs rattle windows and minds,
Sun searches for sunflowers,
Fears freeze running feet.
The deadly quiet
Screams for help.
Earth flattens over me.

Blue and yellow flags
Full of hope,
Crush the red star.
Snow melts under tanks,
Sunflowers refuse to wilt,
Emptied streets cry witness.

February—Los Angeles 2022

February doesn't disappoint. T-shirts suffice to tread through the semi-rough sand. A broken shell scrapes my foot. I pick it up, muse for a moment where it may have traveled from, then toss it, let it pinch someone else's foot. Aimlessly moving on, some waves play catch with me as the sea spreads, scoops up a bit of sand, drops tangled seaweed remnants.

The wetter the sand, the further I follow its warmth, still surrounded by the ocean's music, like an orchestra practicing a symphonic piece. The rhythms of the waves a steady companion to my ambling thoughts, they slowly ease my endless questions. I am comforted by the limitlessness of the sea—it mirrors my persistent search for answers. The certainty of sun, sand and sea remaining here soothes my unease, assures me of a quieted mind.

February—Ukraine 2022

I shiver this balmy February evening watching the news. Russia invaded Ukraine. As the images of Russian tanks roll by, memories of October 1956 cloud my vision. Tanks creak on the cobblestoned street, gunshots pop, too many for me to count. I am in the cellar of my Budapest home, together with our neighbors and their son, Tamás. He and I often walk to school together. As for beds, the grownups give us lounge chairs that by now have lost their summer smell. My parents can't seem to stay put. They alternate going up to the apartment but will not allow me to go with them. I know they are listening to the radio, but they don't tell me what they hear.

Watching the news now, I am overwhelmed by my response. I can't stop crying; I can't turn off the news. I have told the story of those long-ago October days many times to many people. I never cried, it was part of my childhood, my past, leaving various countries and homes, friends, and lovers. But the news of the 2022 Russian invasion strikes me like lightning, opens deeply buried feelings that ache to be freed.

Never Again—Ukraine 2022

"Never again," we said to the world.
The world listened for a short time,
Until it started to forget.
It became restless to
Have power, to rule.
Power corrupts.
Goodwill ends,
Goodwill
Dies.

Never Again—Israel 2023

"Never again," we said to the world.
The world listened for a while,
Until it forgot.
Thirst for power upends the balance,
Foes resurface.
Complacency our hubris,
Fight for survival our primal imperative.
We renew our promise:
"Never again!"

PRESERVING
HOLOCAUST STORIES

Translations

Testimonials

Postcards

Translations

My homeland was torn away from me, but I carried my mother tongue along. In the new land I learned a new language, adapted, and adjusted until the unknown became familiar. My first ten years in Budapest transformed into a prologue to my Viennese adolescence. I wore the new language like a native, my childhood known only to a few.

Settling into adulthood, I reluctantly followed my parents to another country, the New World. Learning English was easier than learning to call Los Angeles home. I've become masterful at readjusting and reinventing myself.

Bits and pieces of the far away decades slip out occasionally from deep inside me. Like pages ripped from a book, I sometimes dare to reassemble the parts, but stop before the whole comes together.

Year after year, the past keeps pulling at me, memories escape and refuse to be locked up. Secrets, revealed only to a few, become my steady companions. They urge me to free them, let them sing and dance.

A vague but steadily nagging quest leads me to the Holocaust Museum. My language skills are welcome. I translate German and Hungarian documents related to Nazi Germany and the Holocaust. The search for the right word doesn't remain a mechanical exchange of languages, but draws me to explore my own history. The more I learn from these documents, the more they connect me to myself and my family. I have no witnesses, no document from my heritage to turn to. I am compelled to become a voice for those who want to know about their family's past. I translate personal documents, testimonials, letters, and post-cards. This archeological dig not only enables those who search to reconstruct a life that was destroyed, but also preserves it for future generations.

Excavating these stories urged and encouraged me to give voice to the past that has haunted me.

Testimonials

Holocaust survivors have given video testimonials to various institutions worldwide. The Shoah Foundation in Los Angeles began collecting in-person interviews in 1994 and their archive contains tens of thousands of video testimonies in multiple languages. I contribute to this endeavor by translating Hungarian and German videos.

Survivors' ages range, their memories vivid of certain experiences and hazy of others. One man is 100 years old, born just a few years after Hungary's independence from the Austro-Hungarian Monarchy. One woman is 83, she has witnessed her hometown being traded back and forth between Romania and Hungary. Another woman is 87, grew up in Bamberg; her parents told her when Germany was united and freed from Prussia's rule.

Why do I painstakingly translate every word these survivors entrust to me as they speak into a microphone? Whether German or Hungarian, my English translation will be transcribed, indexed, and safeguarded in various computerized records.

As I hear these testimonials, the past hundred years of European history become more vivid, more my own. I listen to their stories as voices crack, are muffled by suppressed tears, and sometimes fade away as they search for a word, a name, a date. Historic figures, cities and villages are often unknown to me.

After many hours watching their faces, tilting their heads, clearing their throats, I become increasingly more familiar with their lives. I hear their accounts of surviving deportation, concentration camps, labor camps, ghettos—and building new realities.

Listening to them in either German or Hungarian affects me deeply as it connects me to my mother tongue, my childhood, my years as a hidden Jew. I identify with their home country, with expulsion, with fleeing homes, and with being a refugee. The language that is so thoroughly embedded in my innermost self is the bridge to these strangers who I see only to the extent that a camera focuses on them.

I am an anonymous listener, a secret observer. I know they want to tell their story, want to be heard. I believe their story needs to be known and no language barrier should stop any curious mind from learning about the past, about human resilience, and individuals' place in history.

Postcards

In addition to Hungarian and German videos, I translate Hungarian and German documents, letters, and postcards from the Nazi era for museums to safeguard and provide access for people to retrieve them.

Often, I cannot decipher the words I translate. The ink has faded on postcards that have been stored in boxes for decades, their original guardians unknown. Words obscured by an official stamp "Censored". Words outmoded, words in different languages. Words in a variety of alphabets and handwritings. Words that are code words: cold, snow, and a promise of sunshine hint at various levels of living conditions. To reveal one's state of health, food words like cabbage and turnip are fitting stand-ins. A postponed trip signals a promise to remain in the current place. Code words that speak of fear and longing, hope and hunger.

Postcards with a postal stamp of a country that became a symbol for hatred and murder; of countries whose names and borders have changed; of place names not known any longer and names too faint to read. Return addresses include name, prisoner number, camp name and block number.

Postcards crisscrossed the globe—Europe, Cuba, Shanghai—searching for family members separated, missing, seeking solace. Regardless of time and place, the captives always asked for news from the outside world, news of relatives and hope for return mail.

Once translated and archived, these stories, these lives are exhumed to honor their wish—to live on.

OLD WORLD

Third Grade Pioneers, Hungary 1953

Summer on the Danube 1955

Budapest 1957

Learning German 1957

Meeting Family 1962

English Language Summer Camp 1963

Third Grade Pioneers, Hungary 1953

Blue scarfs knotted under white shirt collars; our uniform put all young elementary school children on an equal level. We were the young pioneers who would make our socialist-communist country proud.

My nanny, Annus, picked me up from school since my mother worked and I was told my father had a job in the countryside. She was always eager to hear what I learned that day and I excitedly told her my teacher said that Rákosi (the Hungarian Communist Leader) was our father. Annus yanked my arm, stuck her thumb under my chin, bent down so low that her breath swiped at my eyes, and said in a loud whisper, "You have a father, and his name is not Rákosi."

I didn't know then that the teacher's words were from a script that every teacher was compelled to recite. I also didn't know then that the family who moved in with us was installed by the Hungarian State Security Agency to act as informers on my mother's activities. The aim was to accuse her as an accomplice to her husband who was alleged to be a spy. But I welcomed their young daughter, finally a playmate for me.

Evenings I had my mother to myself. I had forgotten about Rákosi, but I was eager to ask her about something that happened later. As she tucked me in, I held onto her hand, and she stayed.

"Mommy, how can I give my teacher a pair of nylon stockings?"

"Why would you want to do that?"

"Because that's what Mari did today."

My mother's eyes widened, and the green flecks drowned in a sea of amber. She still held my hand, she didn't move. I worried. Did I tattle on Mari?

"We can't do that." It sounded like she was rehearsing in her head what else to say. I waited but she stayed quiet.

I wanted her to tell me more, so I said, "Why not? Mari and Kati did it. And the teacher put the stockings in her bag and whispered something to the girls and then hugged them."

She let go of my hand, her fingers like reading braille on my face, a broad smile crinkled the corners of her eyes. "It's good that the teacher is happy. And all you need to do is study well." She brushed the hair out of my forehead and kissed me on both cheeks. "Sleep well my precious."

For several days I watched my classmates as they filed past the teacher's desk. I was relieved to see that no one else brought nylon stockings. My blue scarf and I blended in again.

• • •

Snow had melted, we played hopscotch in the schoolyard when Ildikó almost knocked me over.

"Your father is a jailbird," she yelled, ran off and huddled with her friends.

I didn't know what jail was, and I didn't know what a bird had to do with my father. I spent many hours studying the small black and white photograph on my mother's nightstand. Dark, almost twinkling eyes looked at me, lips parted a bit, ready to tell me a story. I saw nothing birdlike in my father's face.

I waited until Sunday, the only day my mother wasn't at work, to finally get an answer to that puzzling word. We had walked to the streetcar stop on the way to visit friends. I held her soft hand that was warmer than a mitten. I leaned into her so close that her black wool coat tickled my cheek.

"Mommy, what is a jailbird?"

She turned around so fast that her hat few off. She gripped my arm.

"Where did you hear that?"

"Ildikó told me that Daddy is a jailbird."

She pulled me to face her, her fingers like claws on my shoulders. Her mouth opened and closed like a fish gasping for air, or choking on words stuck in her throat. She squinted her eyes, some spittle dribbled down her chin.

"Ildikó doesn't know what she is talking about.

Sometimes children say things just to sound smart without knowing what the words mean."

I've never seen her so angry. We never talked about this again.

The next day in school my blue scarf choked me, but I didn't dare to loosen it.

A year later my father came back. My playmate and her parents moved out. My classmates included me in their play.

Two years later the revolution broke out and we burned our blue scarfs.

Summer on the Danube 1955

The anticipation of a boat ride
To summer camp crumbles
On the gravelly ground under my feet.
I squeeze my nanny's hand,
Her sweet soft hand that always finds me.
My mother's words swirl around my ears,
Words whose tentacles fight
Whether to grab or to chase me.
My father wraps his arm around my mother,
Her voice stills.
He pulls me close.

He disappeared for five years,
The government took him away.
In secret. At night.
Apologies and restitutions
Uncover the lies.
As compensation it offers
A gift for a free summer camp.

My father's chocolate eyes don't melt
The anger on my tongue.
The swirling smoke from his cigarette,
Only an excuse for my tear-soaked eyes.
Years ago, my mother banished me,
To stay with my nanny to keep me safe.

Now my parents send me down the Danube,
So they can finally be alone, again.

Budapest 1957

With a sudden jerk, the train leaves the station. My chest heaves trying to steady my breath, I don't bother wiping the tears. I swat away my mother's hand, my father's sonorous voice like a muffled roar in my ears. Why are we on a train? Why is it just the three of us? Why was my nanny left on the platform? My tears are slowly drying, houses and trees like blurred statues disappear past the train's window.

"We'll be in Vienna in about two hours," my mother says.

Vienna? What is that? Why? There are several strangers in our compartment. Everyone, including my parents is whispering, heads bent, staring at nothing. One man's face seems frozen as he watches the door. Who is he waiting for?

"When we get off the train, stay close to us, hold my hand." My mother's voice calm but seemingly from far away. "You'll hear people talking in German, don't worry. Just stay right next to us."

We start walking across the white marble floor, I hear German everywhere. I know a few words, but in the midst of the crowd and clatter of voices, I feel like I'm drowning.

High up on the walls, huge pictures of foods and clothes are displayed all around this enormous room, lit up in bright colors. I try to decipher the words and one startles me: K-A-K-A. It glows in dark brown, but the last letter "O" is just a black outline. KAKAO—the hot chocolate I drank this morning! The illuminated sign is talking to me, reading my thoughts, spelling out my confusion, fear, and sadness.

Learning German 1957

To learn a new language,
In the summer of 1957,
My parents sent me to unknown people,
In an unknown place.

A childless couple in the Austrian mountains,
Desperate for money, took me in.
Those few weeks have shrunk to a single image.

Alone in an attic room, my cries unheard,
My tears unseen, my body superfluous.
I learned enough new words
To go to school,
But too few to name the flood of emotions
Bouncing off the walls, like a bird
Looking for an open window.

Swallowed screams and unanswered pleas
Tucked away safely,
Until I learned another language—
The language of memory.

Meeting Family 1962

My aunt and uncle, whom I've never met, are coming from Los Angeles to Austria. I have seen their handwriting on crisp-soft, almost see-through, air mail stationary. Seen my parents hold the paper steady, which tried to fold in on itself like someone nodding his head. A gentle twist of the wrist straightened up the paper and the silent reading continued. Often, I was asked to write a few words when they were done with their reply. As was my habit I obliged, muttering my annoyance, warding off a useless argument.

I told my friend Eva that I have to go on a trip with them. She listened to my tears of anger and asked me to send her postcards. My father hasn't seen his sister in fifteen years. After the war, he went back to Budapest to build a better world. She went to Los Angeles to have a better life. They reunite here, in Austria, the country that is historically a mediator between East and West.

I walk up the path to our house and there is a strange car in the driveway. Next to my father's Skoda this large black vehicle looks like a mistake. Approaching the living room, I hear voices I don't recognize. "Come in, look who is here!" This man and woman don't look like the picture in the family album. Their clambering voices push against the walls, the room feels too small, and I can't decide where to sit. It's the middle of the week, the middle of the school year, and I am off on a trip. Tuli and Zsuzsa hug me. "Please don't use 'aunt' and 'uncle' and drop the formal way of addressing us. We are used to that living in America," says Zsuzsa. This new rule is as strange to me as their incessant chatter, and I wish I was back with my friend at school.

"I'll drive," Tuli says. He taps my father's shoulder who now looks shriveled and thin, and quietly slips onto the passenger seat.

We cross the Alps, head into Switzerland and on to France. Those few days before we arrive in Cannes play like a foreign movie. We stop for lunch but don't eat a full meal. I taste caviar and shrimp, artichoke and cheeses that are soft and spicy. Dinners last for hours in elegant restaurants, several courses are served; some we eat, some we pick at. Before the red and white wine, drinks arrive in glasses of shapes I have never seen. We don't stay in hotel rooms but in suites where the bathroom is bigger than my room at home, the towels like thick fluffy sheets, warmed on towel racks.

As I walk on the boardwalk in Cannes, I watch the ocean. With each wave that rolls in, another year of my past disappears and reemerges. The changes from Hungarian to German, from Budapest to Vienna, seem like a half-forgotten memory. This new trip is an onslaught of the strange and unexpected. How can I write all that on a postcard?

English Language Summer Camp 1963

His blue eyes out-blue the sky,
His smile more question than play.
To fall in love took only one day.

His German more surprising
Than the cold of the ocean,
His breath a magic tease on my neck,
His lips teach me to kiss.

I toss the English lessons
Into the ocean.
The waves silence all questions,
Our embrace a shadow in the sand.

I leave no footprints
On this rock-filled beach.
I know the now,
I feel it, I taste it,
And clutch it
Before it morphs into memory.

OLD WORLD REVISITED

Berlin 1974

Yugoslavia 1974

Mauthausen 1987

Vienna 2001

Budapest 2009

Shoes on the Danube Bank 2009

Berlin 1974

We crisscross Berlin's cobblestone streets, a stop on our post honeymoon exploration. Hearing German all around, an unseen weight falls off my back. The words so effortless, they wrap around me like a familiar coat. English, almost as new as our love, is still a stranger whom I can't yet trust.

We measure our histories against the sights along the road. A competition, like a buzzing mosquito, wiggles its way between our shoulders. I tread more forcefully, spot a new shimmer in his translucent blue eyes. I wait to hear the words he is sifting through in his head: "This is just like America except with coffee houses."

I swallow, let go of his hand. I walk away.

Yugoslavia 1974

As we walk back for lunch, I tell my husband of the time I was with my friend on this same beach. We were first year students at the University of Vienna and for spring break we came here. Train travel was easy and cheap. Five days in Dubrovnik was an exciting adventure for naïve teenage girls.

Now, my husband and I stay at a hotel that includes all meals. The dining room is crowded but we find a table for two. The long beach walk left us hungry and tired. All the windows are open, the breeze helps dry our sweaty faces. This is Yugoslavia before it was chopped up into eight independent states; before screens on windows shut out bugs, before air conditioners accommodated tourists.

The tablecloth is thick, worn linen that may have been white years ago. Its fraying edges hang just above my knees. There is no menu to choose from, a predetermined meal allows for everyone to have the same lunch. The chef must be a cook who learned the art of creating meals from his peasant mother. It varies daily by substituting potatoes for beans, cucumbers for beets. Pork is either fried or baked, depending on whether the oven works or not. The brown bread is always fresh, slices thick and uneven determined by the kitchen knife. The hotel caters exclusively to foreign tourists, yet we resort to sign language when we want our water glasses filled.

We don't need to request coffee; it comes thick black in tiny espresso cups accompanied by white sugar cubes in a round tin container.

"I wish I could find espresso spoons at home," I complain.

"Do you like these?" Murray asks.

"Yes," I shrug and look around. He slips the two spoons into his palm, reaches in his pants pocket, pulls out a tissue and blows his nose. He signals with his eyes for me to stay quiet.

"Don't worry, the secret police are not waiting for us," he assures me, correctly guessing my deep-rooted fear.

Mauthausen 1987

On our way to Israel, we stop in Mauthausen to help our children understand their history. We travel by train from Vienna. I watch the outside rush by: forests, castles, empty fields. My children interrupt their play and listen to the German station names I read out loud. The disappearing landscape and the steady rumble of the train evoke the image of my mother. She was on a different train. She didn't know where it would take her, didn't know why, didn't know whether to hope or to despair.

"Are we there yet?" My daughters interrupt my faraway thoughts. They are very quiet when we traipse around freshly mowed acres of grass, tattered wooden barracks, and broken concrete structures. They have heard the stories, but they are unable to imagine the smell of rot, the unnamable stench drifting up from chimneys.

I move away, I need to be alone as my mind's eye sees the cadavers. Hears the screams, the pleas. The barking dogs. The crack of the whip. I feel the snow on shriveled bodies, the electric fence that sears the skin.

I stop to tell my daughters about the miracle of luck. I tell them of their grandmother's past.

In the summer of 1944, Rezső Kasztner, the clever Hungarian Jewish lawyer negotiated with Adolf Eichmann, "Hitler's Master of Death" and agreed to a trade deal: trucks in exchange for Jews. That summer, mass arrests and deportations of Hungarian Jews rushed to comply with the "Final Solution". My mother and three remaining members of the Friedländer family were apprehended, herded onto a truck, onto a train and dumped in the Bergen Belsen concentration camp. Some months later, they followed an order to get onto another train. My mother learned, many years later, that the train she was on was the one that Kasztner had negotiated secretly to transport Jews to Switzerland.

Kasztner's clandestine scheme must not become just a page in history books. My mother must not become just a number amongst those who survived.

The girls turn silently to Murray. I am glad they don't say anything now. We continue along the walkway. Signs in many languages, placards, exhibits, lifeless assemblages stare at me. The children seek refuge holding their father's hands. "Can we leave yet?"

I stop one more time at the exit. I do not turn around; I walk to catch up with my family.

Vienna 2001

The train's tempo tapers as I approach Vienna. Blurred houses, shadowy trees gradually retake their familiar shapes. Place names at the stations—Baden, Mődling—words that come alive after years of half-forgotten memory. I say them out loud, roll them around in my mouth to help me find the almost-lost taste. Their sound a melody that stirs in my throat, tightens my chest.

Decades passed, years lived, never to be relived. Events float around like ghosts. Have I ever said *kaddish*? No, just allowed time to dim what was, bury the memories like shovel loads of dirt piled on a casket.

I get off the train, wander around the cobblestoned streets, greet new buildings that have sprung up. Listen to the language, a language that now feels like seeing a sepia photo of an old friend. I search the faces in the streetcar, expect to find those only I knew, the ones I have discarded many years ago. Images appear and disappear, like shuffling a deck of cards. I catch them, I see them as through the wrong end of binoculars, sharper, yet far away.

This is not my first trip back home. After each visit, the past feels closer, it envelops me like a familiar coat, a coat outgrown, too tight.

Budapest 2009

A family trip to Budapest with our two daughters, their spouses and our one-year-old grandson is nostalgia wrapped in learning about a legacy. I lead us through a city that was my childhood home, a city whose sounds feel like a long-forgotten caress.

To show the apartment I grew up in, we take the yellow streetcar that now has padded seats and automatic doors. Through the windows I see landmarks that talk to me, surrounded by a language that only I speak.

We cross the playground with the same swing that knocked me down as a small child. The sandbox is still there, where my father met me and carried me upstairs. I push the images away and point to him. He is now meeting us at the entrance of my long-ago home. The stately gray building is unchanged, stories behind its thick walls ready to be released.

I walk over to my father. "You see the balcony on the second floor?" We both remember that day, September 1, 1954, when he stood on the balcony waiting for me and my mother coming home from my first day of the new school year. We were strangers to each other. It took many weeks to fill in the truth of those five years. Now we are both quiet, hearing the noise of my family's chatter, unable to listen.

I turn to our little group, motioning to go in. We walk up to the second floor. I don't read the name plate next to the doorbell. I didn't practice what to say to the stranger who now lives here. The words tumble out. I explain, I apologize, I watch the suspicion slowly leave her face. She understands my silent plea, asks no questions, and invites us in.

We walk down the narrow hallway and stop at the familiar door.

"This was my room," I say.

"It's so small," Deborah, my younger daughter whispers.

How can I tell my American child that this "small" never felt insufficient? It was my comfort, my refuge. Images like an old movie flash by so fast I can't tell if they are in color or black and white. A snapshot stops the silent film: Deborah's room when she was little, a pink desk, matching chair, a bed with its fluffy Barbie doll blanket. Here is my daughter whose features are witness to her heritage, but she cannot place herself inside this room. She reaches for my hand. She feels my aloneness in this crowded small space.

Shoes on the Danube Bank 2009

Shoes scattered alongside the Danube,
Precariously facing the water.
Women's, men's, children's.
Some in pairs, some fallen sideways.
Shoes rusted and emptied of bodies,
Bodies the river carried away.

Sixty pairs of shoes, sculpted of iron,
Clinging to the stony promenade.
Sixty pairs—a stand-in
For the thousands missing.

Shoes without laces,
Laces used to tie bodies together,
To save bullets
And ease the executioners' task.

Shoes with their open spaces
That once held legs running too slow
To escape their persecutors.
No graves—just shoes agape
Now filled with flowers
And tiny rocks to remember.

An artist's vision of those
Who'll never need shoes again,
Whose blood turned the river red,
In a cold winter,
In 1944.

*Memorial created by film director Can Togay
and sculptor Gyula Pauer 2005*

Photo: Nikodem Nijaki
Shoes on the Danube Promenade - Holocaust Memorial

NEW WORLD

The New World 1965

New Food—Los Angeles 1969

Boston 1971

The New World 1965

My cousin in Los Angeles is getting married. My parents send me to represent them.

High school graduation celebrations over, the unknown lies ahead. With a tearless good-bye at the Vienna airport, I am ready to meet my family, most of whom I've never seen. Expectation and curiosity keep me company on the long flight. My seat neighbor tires of the quiet.

"Where are you going?"

"To Los Angeles."

"LA is big. Where, what part?"

"Encino." I prefer to be rude and not make small talk with this stranger. I squeeze closer to the window. Clouds swim past, their whiteness in the sky-blue air stirs up a memory of airmail envelopes. Envelopes that contain stories of a place and people that previously existed for me only on paper. Other images float by, dissolve as I wake up. I reach for bits I can almost capture, but they dissolve into the void.

My body feels the rattle of the plane before my mind can catch up. I try to invoke the vanished memories when an unseen voice announces that we will land in Los Angeles in twenty minutes. Black nothingness outside the window awakens anticipation and apprehension. My chest muscles respond to my worried thoughts. Tiny sparkles scatter through the black night, they grow and multiply as the plane races over them. I feel the descent, and under me the world is ablaze, an ever-widening glow from millions of giant lightening bugs that illuminate buildings, trees, and cars. A rough thump signals we have landed.

I walk along with the mass of people. Around me everything is too bright, too crowded, too loud. An incessant flow of words I can only pick at sweeps me forward. I scan for signs. I breathe more easily when I spot the picture of a suitcase with an arrow pointing ahead. With the luggage heavy in my hand, the red exit letters are my guide. A sea of people is lined up behind a half-wall, arms swinging like flagpoles, voices covering all octaves.

"Zsuzsika!" I hear my name but can't locate the sound yet. It gets louder, I spot their faces. I wave my free hand and slowly weave my way to my aunt and uncle.

New Food—Los Angeles 1969

I walk on unfamiliar streets,
Learn another new language.
Acres of desert and palm trees
Blur the memory of chestnut trees
Along wide avenues.
I meander through the September heat,
Across a vast LA campus.
Eerie quiet, my only companion.

Classmates invite me to join them
For an afternoon snack.
They are patient with my faulty English,
I pretend I understand their jokes.

"Peanut butter sandwich?"
"Sure."
I don't know what I've agreed to.
Too embarrassed to ask, I wait.

My friend Mark pulls a plastic bag
From the refrigerator,
Its multicolored polka dots
Roll around like balloons that lost their strings.
He takes out several cottony slices of bread,
Dips a gray plastic knife into a jar filled with
A semi-melted milk chocolatey paste.

He spreads it on a piece of bread
And covers it with another slice.
I hold it in my palm,
Careful not to squeeze that sponginess.

Watching the others, I see my father in the kitchen,
Many years ago, just the two of us.
He hugs a loaf of brown bread against his chest,
Cuts off a thick slice.
He grabs a glass jar from the pantry,
And with a blunt metal knife
Smears some of the creamy soft lard,
Sprinkles it with ruby red paprika
And a few grains of salt.
He lights a cigarette, tells me about his day.

The English chatter brings me back to my friends.
I hesitate to bite into the snow-white sandwich.
I try to hide my panic.
A glob of something sweet
Sticks to the roof of my mouth.
My tongue scrapes at it in a silent effort to loosen it.
No one notices my struggle to swallow.

Years will pass
Until I make peanut butter sandwiches
For my children,
Licking the brown sticky mess off the knife.

Boston 1971

Someone's living room, they are all strangers to me; they are all almost strangers to each other. It's a "social", the new residents' class and their partners—spouses, lovers.

"Hi," he says.

I face him. His eyes curious, his mouth ready for questions.

"Where are you from?"

The same question, wherever I go.

"Europe."

This should be enough to end the conversation, but he insists.

"Where in Europe?"

What do you care? They call it small talk. Words exchanged that will not be remembered, extracted to comply with social norms.

"Eastern Europe."

His eyebrows raise up.

Battle of the wills? Yes, I abhor pretense, I ache for substance.

He can't stop. "Where in Eastern Europe?"

I move my whole body toward him, give him my most disarming smile.

"Hungary."

A hand taps my shoulder, my soon-to-be husband extends a hand.

"Hi Alex, I see you and Susan met."

GOODBYES

Goodbye to My Nanny 1957

Goodbye to My Mother 1987

Goodbye to My Father 2015

Goodbye to My Cousin Orit 2017

Goodbye to My Nanny 1957

Is it my breath
That echoes my screaming sobs
That clouds the window?
Is it my tears that distort the face
On the other side?
The face of my beloved,
Who kept our parting a secret,
To let me go into the Free World
I neither needed nor craved.

Goodbye to My Mother 1987

She is unable to speak, unable to walk. She lies in bed, in her home and waits—waits for what? Weeks ago, her world crumbled when a massive stroke muted her. Like my old dolls, dressed up, hair in place, eyes move in sync with her head turning.

Decades of continuous emotional divide, a silent agreement between us. It has grown steadily like water overflowing in a plugged-up sink. Guilt and pity walk me to her bedside. I strain to tell her some minutia of my daily routine. Her face a human mask on a white pillow. My monologue and thoughts fade. The silence echoes in the room. I imagine myself inside an avalanche, unable to stop rolling down while the snow envelops me and grows ever faster, obliterating all sound. I sit up, lean forward, touch the blanket where I guess her hand must be.

"It's ok, whatever was in the past, stays in the past."

I watch her face, lips immobile. Tears slowly wind their way down her protruding Slavic cheek-bones. She understands.

It will take my unwept tears many years to transform into quiet memories.

Goodbye to My Father 2015

I came here, hoping to catch
Some of what I knew, I loved, and now lost.

I came here hoping not to smell disease
Or taste stale bread.
I wanted once more to feel
Our harmonizing dyad,
Before it floated away.
Floated through the yellowed curtains
That exhale his cigarette smoke.
Touch the rows of orphaned books,
Hear their words clatter on the typewriter.

In the closet
His wooly cardigan dangles from a hanger,
Its front wide open, waiting.
I ache to close the buttons to hide the emptiness.

An emptiness that I take with me,
To fill it with crumbs of memories.
Memories I can unpack when longing
Will darken my world,
When memories will lift the curtain of tears.
I go to see his empty room.
His cremated body now in a box
I don't want to hold.
His final Marxist tenet to spite Judaism.

Goodbye to My Cousin Orit 2017

I can finally go,
Orit said yes.
On the long flight
I argue:
Maybe, if, but, no, no.
Like trying to swat at a fly,
The answer escapes.

The airport abuzz with people—
People who run, talk, laugh.
All signs are in Hebrew, English, Arabic.
In the taxi I try not to think
Whole words, only fragments.
My throat is parched from silent,
Incessant questions.

The dog barks as I open the gate.
The door is unlocked,
No one around.
I follow the voices upstairs.
The IV-stand next to her bed
Like a stalk stripped bare
In a forgotten field.

Her smiles squeeze through
The straining chest.

Every day more blood,
Every day less words.
I hold her hand,
Can't let it slip away.
I tell stories from long ago
Until there is no tomorrow.

MEMORIES

Golden Years

Every Wrinkle Has a Story

Now

History

Nightlife

Golden Years

I hear the steady knock of time,
It passes past,
Like a marathon runner
Who leaves no footprints.

Memories erupt like
Faded photographs, their backs blank.
Dates, names, a guesswork
Based on almost forgotten fragments.

Memories appear like a
Surprise package,
Without a return address.
I marvel at what's forgotten,
Hold on to scattered pieces,
Assemble them into a book
That lost its cover,
Title and author missing.

Now pleasure comes in miniatures.
Whispering breeze replaces fiery storms.
Tender kiss echoes unbridled love.
A duet of laughter, witness to
Enchanted happiness.

Morning arrives like an accidental guest,
I feast on its presence, make no demands.
Night will stop a tomorrow.

Every Wrinkle Has a Story

Sometimes I am horrified looking in the mirror. Yet, after closer examination I realize those lines are my memory bank.

The deep crease across my cheek is from that long ago fear I can still feel; all those lines surrounding my eyes are witness to happy laughter; pursing my lips, the lines reflect kisses and caresses; lines of all sizes and depths crisscross my forehead, mirroring endless hours of searching for answers.

I would never want to get rid of all these wrinkles. I would never get rid of my memories.

Now

Memories bounce around like in an old home movie—a staccato followed by a full stop, rushing to a vivace.

A loud siren from not too far away screeches for too long. It is not coming for me yet, is it? *No, I am still here.*

Furrows engraved in my face, shriveled skin appears and fades with every move, like an accordion playing a waltz. *I can still dance.*

My heart's drumbeats accompany me when I cross the street, my eyes fastened on the blinking green light. *I can still walk.*

I float when I hug my children. Butterflies swarm in my belly when my man kisses my cheek. *I can still feel.*

I am calmed by the waves of the ocean; its magic plays a solo until it gets overwhelmed by a full orchestra. *I can still hear.*

The night sky bursts with shimmering stars, their light full of promise. Bees encircle my roses; their faint fragrance foretells the sweet taste of honey. *I can still hope.*

History

History, mine, with all its real and
Imagined memories, haunts me,
Like "Goldberg Variations".
A range of emotions
Weave through me unchained.
I let it flow,
Memories
Of mine
Alone.

Nightlife

The embers of childhood images still flare up,
They may yet revive the flames.
I adored my father's intellectual sensibilities,
His aristocratic charm
And his free-flowing warmth.
I pushed away my mother's scientific mind,
I learned to admire her unwavering loyalty,
Her ironclad love
She only rarely allowed to surface.

Young adulthood knocked on curiosity,
Sent me on a long trek to discover
History and my heritage.
I gathered bits and pieces,
Grabbed forgotten words,
Deciphered whispered codes.
I compiled facts long buried,
And reordered them like loose yellowed pages
From a lost book.
Marriage and motherhood, my teachers
Of protectiveness and forgiveness.
I unlocked the gate to my collection
Of resentments and disappointments.

Now many years later,
When longing and a vague ache pulls at me,

I step outside, seek the dark quiet night,
And imagine my parents can hear my thoughts.
With each unspoken word my mind calms.
These solitary conversations never feel lonely,
The ground appears more solid.
The night air sweeps across my tearless face.

ART
INSPIRATION FOR POEMS

Alexej von Jawlensky

Magdalena Abakanowicz

Marc Chagall

Käthe Kollwitz

Inspired by Alexej von Jawlensky

Alexej von Jawlensky

Kleine Meditation: März 1936, Nr. 10
Leidenschaft und Erkenntnis

Öl auf Malpapier
19 x 12.3 cm

"So dark!"
"No," I answer, "he is at peace."

One cheek ruddy red,
Eyelids, drawn like window shades, guard
Silent images in need of a story.
A small frown—a question? A surprise?

Your lined face, like a book lying sideways,
Hides secrets that are
Yours, yours alone.
Your long aristocratic nose,
A legacy from ancient earth,
Turned into graveyards.
Your silent presence is
My solace, my hope.

Inspired by Magdalena Abakanowicz

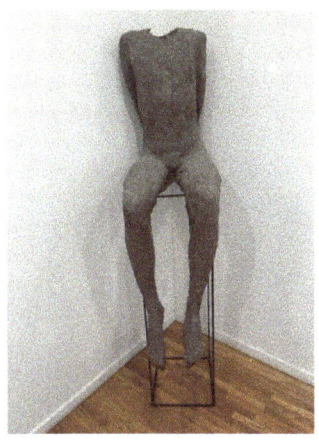

Magdalena Abakanowicz

Loucas

59 x 23 x 15 inches

I didn't search for you—
I felt your call.
You couldn't beckon,
Your arms hidden, your lips silent,
Your eyes vacant, your entire head missing.

You sit on a throne, a stool of iron,
Naked, barefoot.
I dare touch your leg—
Your skin rough, hardened burlap,
Its browns my memory of hot cocoa.
I encircle you on tiptoes—
A scream stifled at your backless hollowed body.

You mock your barbaric killer.
He thought he could eliminate you.
He thought he could disappear you.
He thought you'd never be found.
He thought savagery would win.

He was wrong.

I read your story in your emptied body,
I hear your promise to never be lost.

I didn't know I searched for you
Until I saw you.
I take you home—

Your sightless eyes, your absent mouth—
Your emptied body,
The answer to my search,
My home the answer to your plea.

Inspired by Marc Chagall

Marc Chagall

Blessing of Ephraim and Manasseh

Etching with hand coloring
11 x 9 inches

Your ancient fingers helpless
To children's sorrow
That drips into your lap.
Tears blind to the mocking blue sky
That floats with no remorse.

A stray streak of sunshine on your hand
Like an uninvited guest, refuses to leave.
Your closed lips remember his name,
Your open palms an unwavering cradle
For his shadow.

Inspired by Käthe Kollwitz

Käthe Kollwitz
Sculpture
10 x 8 inches

Your tears dried up,
Eyes swollen from seeing
destruction, denial, despair.

No scream can silence your sorrow,
All words sound empty.
But your hands will continue
To create, to caress, to hope.

MUSIC

Beethoven's 9th symphony
based on the poem
"Ode to Joy" by Friedrich Schiller

Bach's Cello Suites

Coda One—2020

Coda Two—2023

**Beethoven's 9th symphony
based on the poem
"Ode to Joy" by Friedrich Schiller**

The poet's pleas for peace immortalized
In a symphony that speaks every language.

Written words can be erased, but
Sounds, a man's first language,
Can never be silenced.

The deaf composer's soaring voice
Heard by all—
Now dismissed. Again.

Bach's Cello Suites

A single man on a single chair with a cello at his feet on a vast stage in the Hollywood Bowl. An audience of thousands is still. No bottles roll down the steps, no chatter disturbs the expectant quiet. The evening air sucked out all noise from the crowd.

Yo-Yo Ma is the soloist. The program lists one single composition: Bach's six cello suites. No introduction, no intermission. My anticipation grows as I think back on those hours of listening to the music I know so well through radio, records, CDs. Yo-Yo Ma gathers the cello by its neck, leans it against his long legs—an instrument of a woman's curvaceous body with the deep voice of a mature man. From afar they appear as two lovers, a woman at the feet of her beloved who tilts his head listening to her. On the big screen at the Bowl, Yo-Yo Ma sits motionless, eyes closed, his thoughts his alone.

The stillness opens with the gentle notes of the first suite. The music in its familiarity feels like unseen soft hands swirling around my body. No applause breaks the spell, each suite builds on the previous one, an ever-growing union. No need for explanation, the instrument tells a story, composed some 400 years ago. The rhythmic explorations of dances are followed by musical transcriptions of pleading, promises, joys and despair. The layers of notes evoke feelings that over-whelm me unexpectedly.

The Suite No. 5 knocks at my chest, digs deeper with each movement. I don't see images behind my endless tears. I feel sadness and longing that only the music can describe. My chest heaves from sobs I can't let flee past my throat. I allow myself to bathe in a sea of emotions. I can say many words in many languages, but Bach's music speaks a language that only my soul can decipher.

Coda One—2020

Some 30 years ago, I met my cousin Pali in Berlin looking through a folder he held close to his chest, like a fragile baby. "This is about Pál Hermann." He looked at me expectantly. Our grandfathers were brothers whom neither of us knew. Both had been picked up on the street in 1944 and sent to their deaths. Pali, his namesake, has searched for years to uncover his grandfather's past. The man who was a highly regarded cellist and composer. The man who married a Dutch woman who drowned a few years later in the ice-cold North Sea. The man who loved his daughter so much that he let her go to Holland in the hope to save her.

Pál Hermann and his cello crisscrossed the continent until one country after the other was swallowed up by the Nazis. The hunted Jew fled to France but only his cello survived. Kaunas was his last stop.

His grandson, a musician himself, couldn't be sated with stories only. He followed his grandfather's trail, collected sheet music, dates and data. The more material he amassed, the more intent he was on picking the notes off the yellowed papers to let them fill concert halls. Pali believed that this music must not be allowed to decompose like its creator. Music predates words. Music, a universal language, doesn't need translation, only a transcription.

After three decades what remained of Pál Hermann's music was found and restored. His soul is embedded in his compositions. The sonorous deep tone of the cello echoes sorrow, the quiet pizzicatos of the violin whisper bursts of laughter, like shadows from far away. His unfinished symphony was completed by music scholars, analyzing his earlier works and his scattered notes.

Pali assembled his findings into four movements: The composer's life and disappearance; the recovery of his cello; the reviving of his music; concert performances, CDs, videos, and a biography. I now wait to add the coda, see his memorial in Kaunas.

Coda Two—2023

In the Spring of 2023, with the fear of pandemic illness abated and restrictions to travel lifted, Murray and I meet Pali in Venice. The much-celebrated city oozes decay as tourists trip over roller boards, roaming children and fluttering pigeons.

We rely on Pali to get us to the airport. His 6′2″ height and fluency in Italian allows us to move quickly through the crowds and we settle in for a short flight to Vilna, Lithuania. Kaunas is an hour car ride from the capital, the medieval town that has been tossed for centuries between East and West and is now proud of its independence.

A modern highway winds through the hills of the city and climbs up a steep incline to the ancient fortress Kaunas Castle. Attached to it is the "9th Fort" that was turned into a Russian prison in the early years of WW II. Later, as the Germans invaded Lithuania, they expanded the prison and added killing grounds. Following the liberation of Lithuania, the fort was transformed into a museum with a separate section dedicated to the victims of the Holocaust. There, Pali has created a memorial to his grandfather that includes a recording of his music.

Walking through the many rooms separated by massive concrete walls, history is retold. Room after room echoes hopes and heroism. I imagine desperate acts and screams as I search for my great-uncle's memorial. The black and white photograph shows a young man holding his beloved cello—one victim surrounded by thousands whose faces I don't see, whose voices in so many languages I can't understand. Sadness clings to my whole body, my clothes feel leaden. I shiver in the cold of this cavernous room.

I needed to come to Kaunas to complete the journey I had been on with Pali. He has added the final section of the unfinished symphony. I needed to see the site of Pál Hermann's disappearance. For me, looking at this young man and listening to the few chords of his music symbolizes the coda he wasn't allowed to compose—a memorial to let future generations know that music can survive because its power is greater than man's willingness to destroy.

SPECIAL CHILDREN WITH SPECIAL NEEDS

Elliot and The Elevator

Mrs. Sheep

Lucas and Elmo

The Window

Elliot and The Elevator

He is tall for an eight-year-old, with thick blond hair and violet blue eyes. It's our first session for his speech therapy. His teacher warned me that he loves elevators, and he is a "runner". He runs to avoid tasks, runs to perseverate, runs to be alone. He knows his way around the school campus better than me, so I decide to take a detour to my office and bypass the elevator. Suddenly he bolts. Straight to the elevator.

"Elliot, we are going to my office!"

"No, I want the elevator."

"Elliot, we are going to the office, it's not time to go on the elevator."

"Wait for the elevator. I wait for the elevator."

"Elliot, give me your hand."

I reach for his hand, but he pulls away and drops to the floor. His long body stretched out in front of the elevator. I cajole, I sit down, I talk, I am quiet. He doesn't look up, he is silent. I call for help. Two large men arrive, they pick him up, one on his right, the other on his left. They walk him back to the classroom.

Months later we come to an understanding: elevators are not for children.

Before our next session, on our way to my office, a woman walks ahead of us and stops in front of the elevator. The doors open. We stand behind her. She turns around, looks at us puzzled. Elliot watches her get in.

"Elevators are for adults, not for children," he says.

The door closes behind the woman. Tears obscure Elliot's blue eyes, his voice quivers.

"I want to buy an elevator."

"It's very expensive," I say.

"How much money does an elevator cost?"

"Thousands of dollars."

Elliot turns around and I follow him to my office.

Mrs. Sheep

"Hi Mrs. Sheep," Justin's squeaky voice greets me. His chocolate eyes filled with expectation and joy pave a path next to him. I misplaced the farm game he loves, so he cannot clutch the beloved sheep. Unspoiled paper in front, his head turns. Crayon stops in mid-air. He sits still. I watch. I wait, I call his name.

He doesn't move. He listens to what I cannot hear. My nearness wakes him, astonished, he stares at me. His pale face, a sculptor's trophy. Only his eyes tell me he has started on a long trek from far away back to the classroom.

Within moments a smile sweeps his face.

"Hi Mrs. Sheep."

Lucas and Elmo

Lucas walks ahead of me, his therapist. Elmo dangles from his hand along his side. I try to stay close to him, to ensure Lucas will continue down the hallway and we will not end up circling around. Like all buildings on the campus of this school for special needs children, this one too is deceptive. From the outside it is a square, boxy looking, big house. Inside, a circular hallway connects the classrooms. Lucas can't tolerate me holding his hand, so I follow him a few steps behind so that he remains calm and will not run off.

When we approach the EXIT sign above a door, he points to it. "Red exit, green exit," he says, depending on what color light bulb illuminates the sign. He doesn't stop, doesn't even slow his pace, as his pudgy fingers point up and his happy face announces each sign.

Once inside the therapy room, he places Elmo close to him on the table. "Lucas has difficulty staying on task and is highly distractible by his preferred activity," I wrote in one of my reports. As is so typical for children on the autism spectrum, attachment to objects, perseveration with toys and cartoon characters are an essential idiosyncratic behavior. Having Elmo next to him helps Lucas stay calm and be able to attend to the task.

He has made a lot of progress over the past several years I have worked with him. As I watch him holding Elmo's furry arm in one hand and writing spelling words with his other hand, I remember what his mother told me recently.

"I have to tell you a little story. We went to the Sesame Street Show, but could only get seats up in the balcony, and from there Elmo looked like a little red dot. But when Lucas spotted him, he stood up and yelled. "Elmo, I am here, Lukie is here."

I look at Lucas now, as he repeats over and over, "I will follow directions," as he completes the assignment. I marvel at this complex child who does fourth grade work because he knows what is expected of him, but whose emotional equilibrium is maintained by a red puppet that is his joy and comfort.

The Window

His chin juts out about two inches above the window-sill, his blond hair sweeps my shoulder. It's midday, yet the fluorescent lights hum with their cold glare. Eight-year-old Michael and I stand on the smooth linoleum floor, its beige color speaks of nothing. The quiet echoes a smell of emptiness around.

We are on the second floor of the school building, a building that houses goodwill—to teach, to care, to soothe.

On our weekly ritual we witness the gradual disappearance of two old buildings across the parking lot. The remnants of the apartments now abandoned carcasses, the crumbling stucco a faded memory. The backhoe smoothes out the debris.

The powerful jaw of the machinery is a credible replica of a comic book robot. Tightly shut windows create the illusion of watching a silent movie. Yet the California blue sky, the orange metal giant and the solitary palm tree jolts us back to the preparation of the future annex to the school.

"Soon they can start on the new building," I hear myself comment.

"Yeah, they are building the Bonaventure Hotel," Michael says.

He told me that he had watched its construction downtown for several months. All my efforts to convince him that the current construction will not be another Bonaventure Hotel have failed. In his mind, all construction will result in a high-rise building. How long will he rigidly hold on to his certainty? Will it collapse before this building is complete? How devastating will his disappointment be when the new structure does not resemble the glass and steel high-rise? Will he simply lose interest during the long wait? Fascinated, these questions whirl in my mind, and I guide him into the therapy room.

I have never stopped at a building site pondering the end result. Listening to Michael, the hunks of metal come alive, the oversize glob moves about as a resurrected dinosaur, the mess of dirt and rocks ready to form a new image.

I admire the easy fantasy world of this child and his tremendous need to make order out of chaos, to change the unformed into the concrete. I help him learn that destruction is temporary, and he will understand that memory will shiver next to the new unknowable.

TRAVEL

Chengdu, China 2004

Tokyo to Kyoto, Japan 2004

Cuba 2007

India 2013

St. Petersburg, Russia 2013

Morocco 2014

The Gobi Desert, Mongolia 2017

Lake Baikal, Siberia 2017

Hawaii 2022

Chengdu, China 2004

"Chengdu is a small city," our tour guide announces, a city of more than 16 million people. I wonder what the word for "small" is in Chinese? I watch a city bus approach its stop. Before its doors even open, dozens of people rush and push, a clatter of loud high-pitched words compete for speed. Shoving hands eliminate space between bodies. As the doors close, I see masses of people squeezed inside, holding each other up—no need for handrails or hand straps.

I turn to my travel mate. "Now I can breathe again."

Tokyo to Kyoto, Japan 2004

"I'll walk you to the track," our tour guide announces. His tone does not allow for contradiction nor does his bow astonish me any longer—this is the Japanese way. Descending the long escalator, I watch people on the staircase. Even though no one is walking down, dozens of people walk up, strictly on the right side, following the directive on the posted sign.

At the track our tour guide stops at the number 7, etched at the edge of the platform. He points to our ticket that has a bold, black number 7 printed on it. I look around and notice numbers in sequential order along the entire length of the curb. More travelers arrive, all of whom quietly queue up at each number.

The train pulls in. As it stops, the number 7 on the train car is perfectly aligned with the number 7 on the curb in front of me. Single file, passengers get on. I can see, more than hear, shoes moving forward. A whispered "wow" escapes my mouth. I'm comforted by the knowledge that we will get off at number 7 marked on the curb at Kyoto station.

Cuba 2007

We went to Havana in the guise of a medical mission. We explored tourist sights, hospital wards and beach resorts. We capped off the week with a New Year's Eve dinner.

Our hotel concierge wrote down the name of a restaurant he recommended. Note in hand, a cabdriver zigzagged through crowded streets and potholes. The car's radio station drowned out our silent worries.

People in festive party clothes crowded around a dozen tables covered with white tablecloths. None of the New Year's Eve type decorations we expected, but loud rhythmic jazz from speakers greeted us. We were seated by a tall, rotund waiter who unloaded a barrage of incomprehensible words, punctuated by hands twirling and pointing, while a big smile extended to his twinkling eyes. With more mimicry than Spanish we ordered dinner. Our hands imitated swimming like fish, we clucked, we mooed. Each of our attempts he translated into its Spanish equivalent. His laugh was infectious, and we shed our embarrassment.

Almost immediately, three men who had been sitting at a table, gathered around an upright piano and tuned their violins and cello. We guessed them to be in their thirties, dressed in mock tuxedos, open white shirt collars and shiny black leather loafers. The room quickly filled with cigarette smoke and music that brimmed with African rhythms and European harmonies. Their tapping feet were a welcome substitute for a drummer, as they took turns singing solo and in unison. Tables were surrounded by empty chairs—everybody danced, sang, and grabbed us to join in.

Long after midnight we showed our patient waiter the address of our hotel. He read our questioning faces and understood our tortured Spanish. He patted his chest and motioned to make a phone call. The music, the wine and general giddiness erased our concerns. A few minutes later, our waiter waived to us to follow him outside. On the barely lit sidewalk, an elderly man approached us.

"I am his cousin, I'll drive you home."

We were assured by his quite fluent English. He led us to an old, banged up Lada and opened the door for us to get in. The seats were covered in colorful blankets, pieces of packing tape held the rear-view mirror in place, and air freshener attached to the gearshift overwhelmed the smell of old. The driver, who never told us his name, turned to us, "this is my Russian Ferrari."

India 2013

From Delhi to Jodhpur, Udaipur, Jaipur, and Agra to Kanpur, I've lost track of all the temples, Buddhas, beggars and opulent hotels stored in my camera. Now we leave behind the dense crowds, chaotic mass of cars, buses, bicycles, and horse drawn carriages where a deluge of humans and animals fight for space to move and compete for air to breathe.

In Varanasi, the "spiritual capital of India", a guide leads us through dark, deserted alleys. It is late at night, quiet—even a lone cow that trots along makes no sound as he passes us. We wade through a labyrinth of unlit streets; their cobblestones tell of forgotten times.

Voices become more distinct as we approach a large fenced-in yard. Hundreds of women sing, laugh, embrace each other and chant in unison. Only the full orange moon illuminates them and follows us down a winding path.

Across the river, dozens of men are gathered to feed funeral pyres. The black night is painted by glowing golden flames. The steady murmur of the Ganges and the silent sky are witness to the haunting mix of mourning and celebration. Smoke swirls around the pyres, the deep red blaze calls me with its flickering of light and dark. The continuous crackling of the roaring fires echoes my heartbeats, as I listen to the sound of the waves like a gentle adagio.

From afar, amorphous shapes appear as clusters of human forms that bend and bow as the dead disappear in the flames. A heap of discarded saris grows, fed by men's busy hands that follow a rhythm only they can hear. The saris' vivid colors tell the stories of lives lived. The reds speak of love, yellows and oranges of warmth, while the greens and blues celebrate calm, and the whites, purity.

Now, wet saris emptied of bodies drift down the holy river. Some swallowed by the water, some welcomed by the poor who wait in need. I watch. I see. I listen. An unnamable part of me sails across the Ganges as bright yellow flowers mingle with the ashes. Petals of reds and whites surround the vacant spaces as voices chant.

Souls flutter like lightening bugs circling the sparks of the burning logs.

St. Petersburg, Russia 2013

Large oak and pine trees proudly display their thick leafy crowns as we walk along the riverbank. We are ready to browse without our guide and take a break from Russian history.

We spot a modern art museum that is eerily empty, just a few scattered visitors. The exquisite collection distracts me for a while, but as is my habit, I check my surroundings. In the room we had just left, I notice a man, alone, well dressed. I continue exploring the art but every time I turn around, I see the same man, always trailing one room behind us.

I tell Murray that I am convinced we are being followed by a secret service agent. He laughs, reminds me that it's 2013 and Stalin is dead. The longer we stay, admiring the art, the more nervous I get. The more I insist on my suspicion, the more Murray brushes me off.

Making our way toward the exit after about an hour, I lose sight of the man. We leave the museum, walk to a nearby café. After a few meters, I turn around and there he is, keeping his usual distance from us. He finally disappears after we sit down, and I sip my espresso sweetened with the satisfaction that I was right. The date may have changed but Russia has not.

Morocco 2014

Marrakesh

The souk dense, crowded.
Voices tumble over each other,
Vendors and visitors weave through
Throngs of onlookers.

Merchants offer teas,
Their aroma tempts and bewilders.
Rugs and curios sparkle in a myriad
Of reds and blues.
Men and mules carry their wares,
Muezzins' voices, magnified and urgent,
A symphony of unseen chants.
Moccasins scurry to answer the call.

The Sahara

A young nomad leads me atop his camel.
Quiet, steady—wind and sand our companions.
High above, the whirling granules
Filter the sun's glare.
Golden waves in continuous motion,
Mounds of ochre sand rise and flatten.
Shadowless crests and valleys surge and sink.
Warm winds rush, then rest.

I am an intruder in this vast expanse.
My footsteps invisible, no traces left.
Yellow powder crunches between my teeth.
The air sings a melody no man has composed.
It will forever play in my head,
Accompanied by never fading images.

The endless sand piles, the limitless sky
Fill me with weightlessness.
I burst with exuberance and awe.
I crave to fly, lifted up by the wind
To sink into a sea of soft sand.
No sound disturbs the stillness.
A profound calm ferries me through the Sahara

The Gobi Desert, Mongolia 2017

The camel sits motionless.
Legs folded under his belly,
He slowly turns his long, graceful neck,
An aristocrat's glance grabs me.

I hoist myself up, high off the ground,
Cradled between his two humps.
My hands embrace his bristly hairs,
A Mohawk crown on bareback.

My body sways with his slow gait.
We ride past clumps of faded greenery
Sprinkled across a golden sea,
Full of ripples and haze.

I fuse into the camel's boney back.
I feel my skin lift—a sensuous mirage.
The heat envelops me,
My breath dances in the wind's rhythm.

The camel stops, lowers its front legs.
My body tilts forward
In synchrony with his.
He doesn't look back when I leave.

I hike up, I skid, I stumble.
My feet sink into the hot, grainy softness.

The wind wipes off my sweat,
Its whispers and cries tell an ancient story,
That fades and returns,
Like the everchanging field of sand.

I drift through the amber vastness,
Cup some magic granules,
A weightless pond in my palm,
And let them slowly flow through my fingers.
My heartbeat accompanies them home,
As they meld into the caramel expanse.

Lake Baikal, Siberia 2017

A thick forest of deep green pine trees accompanies us to the hotel. The car pulls up to a wooden house that is a tall version of the ones we passed on the long ride.

Our driver and the hotel concierge ask us to follow them. Three stories up, splinters send a warning, creaks tell a soulful cry. Laundry hangs in hallways above a patched once red colored rug.

The large, rusted metal key opens the door to our room. Hot, fetid air spells "stop". A small window's dirty streaks can't obscure the view—an empty field strewn with trash amid dried patches of grass. Lake Baikal may be a myth.

Without stepping over the threshold, we do not accept a "nyet" and ignore the onslaught of Russian we cannot translate. After a brief "stare-à-stare" our driver takes us back to the Irkutsk hotel.

Hawaii 2022

The sun starts to lean toward the horizon as the air remains balmy. Our noisy group of ten wrangles over the dinner choices. A patient waitress listens, scans the table, answers all the questions. The children's high-pitched laughter competes with the adults recounting the day's activities. This Hawaii beach vacation was aborted by Covid-19 two years ago. Now the freedom to be here is like unwrapping a special gift.

The cacophony of the chatter and jostling exuberance unsettles me. I walk away, don't look at the questioning faces. I cross the manicured lawn; my sandals fill with still warm sand, and I stop at the water's edge. I don't remember when my tears started to drip down my face. The endlessness of the ocean conjures up the millions of recently traumatized refugees. I cry for them, for the willful destruction of cities, the raw brutality of the invaders. I know my tears have been dormant for sixty plus years, the sadness that torments me is rooted in long ago events. Reason cannot quiet my suppressed sobs; silent screams are stuck in my throat. My tongue moves too slowly to lick off the salty wetness.

I force myself to turn away from the steady motion of the sea, force myself not to see the blue in the Ukrainian flag as I watch the lavender sky. I scold myself that I indulge in my grief and sorrow. I deafen my ears to faraway bombs striking the concrete and head back to my family.

MUSINGS

Obsession

Countries

Lies

Salty Tears

Music

The Shadow

.

Obsession

Obsession—is it a
Burden or a solace?
Solace to those who need
Every minutia?
Straight jacket for those whose ideas
Soar and scatter in the void,
Impulsive and irreverent?
Obsession: a search for
Never attainable illusion.

Countries

I. Childhood (Hungary)

I am from a country that doesn't share its language with anyone.

I am from a country that terrorized its citizens with show trials and murders.

I am from a country where tanks and guns sent my family fleeing.

II. Youth (Austria)

I am from a country that welcomed refugees. I learned a new language.

I am from a country where I had to hide my religion but was free to speak my thoughts.

I am from a country that became my home until I was uprooted again.

III. Adulthood (US)

I am from a country that was alien in its language, culture, and landscape.

I am from a country that I chose to never leave, where I found love and a lover.

I am from a country where I created a future.

Each country, each language, was like a new coat, the old ones never discarded,

Their colors faded, their textures thinned, their shapes outmoded.

But I will never forget how they enfolded my body.

Lies

How many lies can I tell
Before I can't tell that I am lying?
I was told a lie that my father
Worked in a faraway place.
I was told a lie in school that Rákosi was our father.
I was told a lie in Vienna that I was Protestant.

I lied in different languages,
I lied in different countries,
I lied to escape ridicule, resentment, rejection.

Once an adult, I tried to lie no more.
I unraveled the thick layer.
My body now cold, naked.
My lips loose, words allowed to spill out.

I am in a new country whose language I speak,
But am afraid to talk.
I practice and catch my almost-lies.
Will I ever be without a lie?

Salty Tears

Salty tears of sorrow
Flow in a thin stream down my cheeks.
Some are quick, wet my neck,
Some I lick off the edges of my mouth.
I don't disturb their quiet,
I suppress the sobs.

Salty ocean, a comfort.
The cold water wakes up my body.
Lips closed tight, my breath locked in.
Submerged, I blindly push forward,
Listen to the muted noise.
I imagine the waves dance above me.

My tears follow a path only I feel,
My vision blurry.
The hiccupping sobs mourn the unfinished,
The untried, the unrequested, the unexamined.
I can't sweeten the tears,
I can't still the doubts.

Under water, all thought is to the now.
My body in sync with the rhythm of the waves.
The humming dark in the wetness,
A solace to the haunting questions.
Tears dry up behind closed eyes.
The endless water greets the pale horizon.

I let my body sink into the soft sand,
My eyes adjust to sunlight.
The sun can't dry up my unanswered questions.

Music

When I choke on sadness, it coddles me.
It abates my thirst
When my lips are parched and silent.
It stalls my running, closes my eyes,
And tells me to listen,
So that I can read the dancing notes,
And hear the story I long for.

The Shadow

The Shadow only I can feel—invisible, quiet but always with me, around me, inside me. When did I first feel it? When did I first realize it will always be with me? Like my heartbeat—sometimes I listen to it, sometimes I ignore it.

Days, decades passed—the Shadow became a burden, an invisible foe. I had a sense of being hunted, under surveillance, fleeing. Why? What did I do?

Slowly, shapeless bits and pieces of my past began to fit together. The multiple sorrows of leaving another home, another country, another language. Elusive fragments merged. I gradually acknowledged my Jewish heritage.

The Shadow, once a threatening enigma, morphed into a symbol of my past and eventually became again like my heartbeat—always with me, sometimes painful, often unnoticed. I accept its presence.

ACKNOWLEDGMENTS

My sincere thanks to Martha Fuller for her continued support and encouragement. Her knowledge and wisdom led me to find the right words to convey my belief in the importance and value of memories.

ABOUT THE AUTHOR

Born in Budapest, Hungary in 1947, Susan H. Brown moved to Vienna, Austria in 1957 and emigrated to the United States in 1969. In 1973 she received an MA from Boston University, (German Languages and Literature) and in 1987 she received an MA from California State University, Northridge (Communication Disorders). For several years,she worked as a speech/language therapist. Brown currently lives in Los Angeles, California and translates video testimonials in Hungarian and German for USC Shoah Foundation. She also translates historical documents, letters and postcards from ghettos, concentration camps, and various hiding places, for Holocaust Museum LA. Susan H. Brown's book *Circles: A Legacy* was published in 2020. *Perspectives in Time* is her second collection of poetry and prose.

'